psalms

and

consolations

a jesuit's journey
through grief

Timothy Brown, S.J.

Printed in the United States of America.

ISBN: 0-9668716-7-7

First Edition
10 9 8 7 6 5 4 3 2 1

Edited by Susan Hodges
Design by Kathleen Ryan

resonant publishing

Baltimore, Maryland
info@resonantgroup.com • www.resonantgroup.com

to my mother and father...

table of contents

introduction

—Preface—

In 1998 I was diagnosed with colon cancer. During my illness and year of recovery, I turned to the Book of Psalms as I focused on healing. As fruit of that recovery process, I published Psalms and Compassions, *a compilation of Psalms, prayers, and reflections.*

Since that time, a number of people have approached me requesting a companion volume on bereavement and grief. I had only to reflect on my experiences with the deaths of my parents, friends, and colleagues to know that the Psalms again were the source of greatest consolation.

This book is dedicated to all those left behind in their loss of family or friends, anyone suffering any kind of loss. It is my hope that this small volume helps you bear that grief and brings you renewed hope and faith. Stand strong. Breathe hope. Live faith.

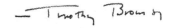

—The Inspiration—

I find in times of loss that the Psalms offer great consolation. I use a wonderful volume, The Psalms with Commentary *by Kathleen Norris. In the Introduction to her volume, she writes:*

The God one encounters in the Psalms is God as human beings have experienced him as both awake and asleep, gloriously present and lamentably absent, and above all, various. A warrior who stands up for us, a mother who holds us to her breast. An eagle sheltering us under her wing, and a creator who brings forth lightning, wind, and rain from the storehouses of heaven. The Psalms work in the way that all great poetry works, allowing us to enter no matter who we are or what we believe, or don't believe; addressing us at the deepest level—what Saint Benedict might term "the ear of the heart." (pp. vii, viii)

I found myself drawn to the language of the King James version of the Psalms. Why the King James version, with its lack of inclusive language, you might wonder? Again, Kathleen Norris puts it so well:

One reader of a Jesuit magazine wrote an angry letter to complain about an article that had prominently featured a quotation from John Donne: "No man is an island." The editors commented that since Mr. Donne had died in 1631 they had no means of inviting him to revise his grammar for the more "inclusive" modern era. To read and appreciate seventeenth-century verse, or the King James Bible, one must favor imagination over ideology, and discover for oneself the inclusivity that is there. But this is an increasingly difficult task in our literal-minded age. (p. xiv)

But many poets who write in English regard the King James as the literary standard by which to judge subsequent translations of the Bible. The story of this translation – so called because it was commissioned by King James I of England early in the seventeenth century—is a story about the power and primacy of vivid language and pleasurable speech, words that hold the attention of the ear and provide physical images pleasing to the mind's eye. The translation has so embedded itself into the English language that most people are unaware that many images and phrases still in use entered the idiom through the King James: 'my cup runneth over,' 'all flesh is grass,' 'on eagles' wings,' 'tender mercies,' 'loaves and fishes,' 'lilies of the field,' 'salt of the earth,' 'through a glass, darkly,' 'where your treasure is, there will your heart be also.' (p. xvi)

So I ask you to join me in praying through the Psalms – in imagery that is poetic but not inclusive in the literal sense of the meaning. The images evoked are vivid and provide a great deal of comfort. Join me in your prayer.

time

—Time—

There are times during the grieving process when we break apart to a gamut of emotions.

There is crying. There are tears – and certainly regrets.

I hold onto something I heard once, that the past is a dream, the future a vision. But the present well lived makes the past a dream of beauty and the future a vision of hope. We learn to live with our remembering – with this dream of beauty, this vision of hope.

—Listing of Emotions—

There is great consolation in praying a litany. I came across this uncritical listing of emotions and realized this list could be used as a litany —

> *"In my admiration,...*
>   *Lord hear my prayer.*
> *In my agony,...*
>   *Lord hear my prayer.*
> *In my love,...*
>   *Lord hear my prayer."*

Through the litany, we become reconciled with our conflicting emotions.

Admiration	Emptiness	Regret
Affection	Envy	Resentment
Agony	Fear	Sadness
Aggravation	Frustration	Shame
Anger	Guilt	Sorrow
Anxiety	Hope	Sympathy
Awe	Loneliness	Tension
Despair	Love	Uncertainty
Doubt	Piety	

—Psalm 77—

1.	I cried unto God with my voice, even unto God with my voice; and he gave ear unto me.

2.	In the day of my trouble I sought the Lord: my sore ran in the night, and ceased not: my soul refused to be comforted.

3.	I remembered God, and was troubled: I complained, and my spirit was overwhelmed.

4.	Thou holdest mine eyes waking: I am so troubled that I cannot speak.

5.	I have considered the days of old, the years of ancient times.

6.	I call to remembrance my song in the night: I commune with mine own heart: and my spirit made diligent search.

7.	Will the Lord cast off for ever? And will he be favourable no more?

8.	Is his mercy clean gone for ever? Doth his promise fail for evermore?

9.   Hath God forgotten to be gracious? Hath he in anger shut up his tender merits?

10.   And I said, This is my infirmity: but I will remember the years of the right hand of the most High.

11.   I will remember the works of the Lord: surely I will remember thy wonders of old.

12.   I will meditate also of all thy work, and talk of thy doings.

13.   Thy way, O God, is in the sanctuary: who is so great a God as our God?

—Time is Eternity—
St. Augustine

Time is too slow for those who wait,
Time is too fast for those who fear,
Time is too long for those who mourn,
Time is too short for those who rejoice,
But for those who love, time is eternity.

Times of sorrow seem interminable. There is the need to remember and rejoice – a great part of this is the remembering of childhood memories. The care of my family.

Care – I felt cared for and that care translated into love for me. That love translated into the center of my vocation. But the sorrow of loss does not easily turn to joy. The eternal name of love – that same love – Jesus, yesterday, today, forever. That love cannot be taken away. There is deep consolation in knowing that love for all eternity.

—Everything is Grace—
St. Therese

Everything is a grace; everything is
the direct effect of our Father's love.

Difficulties, contradiction, humiliation, all one soul's
miseries, her burdens, her needs, everything,
because through them, she learns Humility,
realizes her weakness.

Everything is a grace because everything is
God's gift. Whatever be the character of life
or its unexpected events, to the heart that loves,
all is well.

—A Happy Funeral—

I was moved by this homily given by a fellow Jesuit and friend, Ron Anton, S.J. It speaks of time in a way that gives me consolation.

In China, I am told there are two words for funeral. When one is over 80, there is a different word. The translation of the second word is: a happy funeral.

This is a happy funeral. Mom lived a long life, more than four score and ten years. She was the last of her ten siblings. We no longer have any uncles or aunts on either side. Mom was the last of a generation. She saw not only her children's children, but lived long enough for her children's children to have children.

There is a time for everything. A time for giving birth and a time for dying. This was her time to die.

Already God had started to store her treasures in heaven. Several years ago she started to store more and more memories in heaven. Her mind went gradually. In the beginning it was just small parts of the story that did not make sense but in the end, not pieces but all her mind and memory was stored in heaven. And in recent months the functions of her body also left her. Everything was already in heaven except her heart, which kept on beating. It was for her a time to die.

Even though it was her time to die and we would not wish to prolong her stay among us, here, today, we miss her. Terribly. We are saddened for ourselves and our loss. We miss the sound of her voice, the look in her eyes, the touch of her hand. Both our parents loved us. And we loved them. And they left us with a wonderful gift, a priceless gift — their forever-faithful love for each other. That is a gift no one can ever take from us.

Miss her, yes; but today we also rejoice with her. On the night of her death we told Mom that Jesus will be coming for her. That Dad and her sisters and brothers and her granddaughter, Tammy, would be with him. We told Mom to go home with them. We reminded her that this was the reason she was born. To live forever in the land of love, with God who is love, with Jesus who loved her so he suffered and died for her, with Dad who went before her and to whom she pledged — over sixty years ago — a love that would never die.

We told Mom that she has nothing to fear. God forgave her all her sins and failings. Jesus himself, as St. Paul tells us, was interceding for her. And there was nothing that could separate her from the love of Christ. God's love for each of us was so strong that nothing on earth, nothing in heaven, nothing in life, nothing in death, could keep God from loving her. It was this God who waited on the other side of death's door. It was this

God who waited to hug her and hold her. It was this God who longed to say to her, "Long have I waited for your coming home."

We read to her the Gospel we read here today — with the promise that not one who comes to Jesus, who is baptized into the community of believers, and who lives a life of love would ever die. The kingdom of heaven, the kingdom of love, is like no other kingdom. It has no end. Jesus would raise her up and would live in that kingdom forever.

So today is not a time of sadness. It is a happy funeral. It was her time. She is home now. And there she will live without fear, without pain, in complete and faithful love with Jesus, with Dad, with all those she loved so much.

It is up to us to live from now on so that we too are included in that homecoming.

Margaret Anton
4 October 1911 – 9 March 2002

—In the Twinkling of an Eye—
1 Corinthians 15: 51-55

Behold, I tell you a mystery. We shall not all fall asleep, but we will all be changed, in an instant, in the blink of an eye, at the last trumpet. For the trumpet will sound, the dead will be raised incorruptible, and we shall be changed. For this which is corruptible must clothe itself with incorruptibility, and this which is mortal must clothe itself with immortality. And when this which is corruptible clothes itself with incorruptibility and this which is mortal clothes itself with immortality, then the word that is written shall come about:

"Death is swallowed up in victory.

Where, O death, is your victory?

Where, O death, is your sting?"

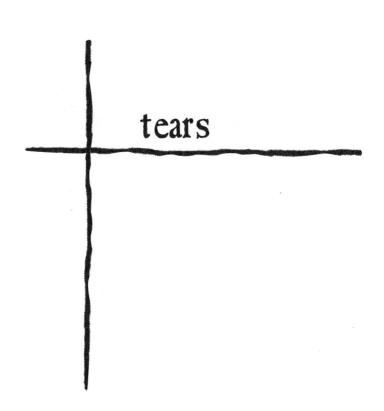

tears

—Tears—

The gift of tears. St. Ignatius experienced tears before and during Mass. From The Spiritual Journal of St. Ignatius Loyola, *translated by William J. Young, S.J.*

March 17, 1554

[T]he Giver of all graces provided such an abundance of knowledge, consolation and spiritual relish, as I said, with tears that were so continuous that I lost the power of speech, so that I thought that every time I named God, Lord, Etc., I was penetrated through and through with a wonderful and reverential respect and humility, which cannot be explained.

Letting the tears flow. The same tears that my parents shed on different occasions. The same tears of joy. The same tears of my sadness going to camp or college. Remembering my own parents' tears in airports and in goodbyes – tears of pride and sadness. A consolation to remember and to think of their own tears.

—2 Timothy 1:4—

I yearn to see you again, recalling your tears, so that I may be filled with joy, as I recall your sincere faith.

—My Life is a Moment—
St. Therese

My life is an instant — a fleeting now.
My life is a moment, which swiftly escapes me.
O my God, you know that
On earth I have only today to love you. Amen.

—Psalm 42—

1. As the hart panteth after the water brooks, so panteth my soul after thee, O God.

2. My soul thirsteth for God, for the living God: when shall I come and appear before God?

3. My tears have been my meat day and night, while they continually say unto me, Where is thy God?

4. When I remember these things, I pour out my soul in me: for I had gone with the multitude, I went with them to the house of God, with the voice of joy and praise, with a multitude that kept holyday.

5. Why art thou cast down, O my soul? and why art thou disquieted in me? hope thou in God: for I shall yet praise him for the help of his countenance.

6. O my God, my soul is cast down within me: therefore will I remember thee from the land of Jordan, and of the Hermonites, from the hill Mizar.

7. Deep calleth unto deep at the noise of thy waterspouts: all thy waves and thy billows are gone over me.

8. Yet the Lord will command his lovingkindness in the daytime, and in the night his song shall be with me, and my prayer unto the God of my life.

9. I will say unto God my rock, Why hast thou forgotten me? Why go I mourning because of the oppression of the enemy?

10. As with a sword in my bones, mine enemies reproach me; while they say daily unto me, Where is thy God?

11. Why art thou cast down, O my soul? And why art thou disquieted within me? Hope thou in God: for I shall yet praise him, who is the health of my countenance, and my God.

—A Tear Evaporates—

A tear evaporates,
A flower on my grave wilts,
But a prayer for my God will heal.
Do not cry my loved ones,
For I am going to join my God,
And await you in heaven.
I die, but my love does not die.
I shall love you in heaven,
As I have loved you on earth
To all those who have loved me,
I ask you to pray for me…
For that is the greatest proof of love.

— *Anonymous*

—Psalm 142—

1.   I cried unto the Lord with my voice; with my voice unto the Lord did I make my supplication.

2.   I poured out my complaint before him; I shewed before him my trouble.

3.   When my spirit was overwhelmed within me, then thou knewest my path.In the way wherein I walked have they privily laid a snare for me.

4.   I looked on my right hand, and beheld, but there was no man that would know me: refuge failed me; no man cared for my soul.

5.   I cried unto thee, O Lord: I said, Thou art my refuge and my portion in the land of the living.

6.   Attend unto my cry; for I am brought very low: deliver me from my persecutors; for they are stronger than I.

7.   Bring my soul out of prison, that I may praise thy name: the righteous shall compass me about; for thou shalt deal bountifully with me.

—Chili Recipe—

A tangible reminder of my mother.
Memories and tears – my mother's chili. The onions made me
cry – I cry and I renew and taste the chili and think of her.

1 lb. Ground Beef
1-20 oz. Kidney Beans
1-46 oz. tomato juice
1 large onion, chopped
1 Tablespoon of chili pepper
1 Tablespoon of sugar
Salt and pepper to taste

Brown hamburger with onion until pink leaves meat.
Add all other ingredients and simmer for 15 minutes.
Serve with oyster crackers.

—Romans 8: 38-39—

For I am persuaded, that neither death, nor life, nor angels, nor principalities, nor present things, nor future things, nor powers, nor height, nor depth, nor any other creature, will be able to separate us from the love of God, in Jesus Christ our Lord.

—Lord, Grant Me a Holy Heart—
St. Thomas More

Lord, grant me a holy heart that sees always what is fine and pure and is not frightened at the sight of sin but creates order wherever it goes. Grant me a heart that knows nothing of boredom, weeping and sighing; let me not be too concerned with the bothersome thing.

my mother

—Psalm 139—

1.   Lord, thou hast searched me, and known me.

2.   Thou knowest my downsitting and mine uprising, thou understandest my thought afar off.

3.   Thou compassest my path and my lying down, and art acquainted with all my ways.

4.   For there is not a word in my tongue, but, lo, O Lord, thou knowest it altogether.

5.   Thou hast beset me behind and before, and laid thine hand upon me.

6.   Such knowledge is too wonderful for me; it is high, I cannot attain unto it.

7.   Whither shall I go from thy spirit? Or whither shall I flee from thy presence?

9.   If I take the wings of the morning, and dwell in the uttermost parts of the sea;

10.   Even there shall thy hand lead me, and thy right hand shall hold me.

11. If I say, Surely the darkness shall cover me; even the night shall be light about me.

12. Yea, the darkness hideth not from thee; but the night shineth as the day: the darkness and the light are both alike to thee.

13. For thou hast possessed my reins: thou hast covered me in my mother's womb.

14. I will praise thee; for I am fearfully and wonderfully made: marvelous are thy works; and that my soul knoweth right well.

15. My substance was not hid from thee, when I was made in secret, and curiously wrought in the lowest parts of the earth.

16. Thine eyes did see my substance, yet being unperfect; and in thy book all my members were written, which in continuance were fashioned, when as yet there was none of them.

17. How precious also are thy thoughts unto me, O God! how great is the sum of them!

18. If I should count them, they are more in number than the sand: when I awake I am still with thee.

These great psalms bespeak life. I am grateful to my parents for the gift of my life.

—The Litany in Honor of Saint Ann—

*The power of the litany – pray for us – the power of repeti-
tion – pray for us. I pray a litany – the repetition, the rosary,
the consolation of prayer. The constant repetition of words can
work a slow but deep transformation of our hearts. At my
mother's wake, we prayed this litany in honor of Saint Ann
and Ann Brown. I think their lives mirrored one another.*

Saint Ann, pray for us,
Offspring of the royal race of David,
Daughter of the Patriarchs,
Faithful spouse of Saint Joachim,
Mother of Mary, the Virgin Mother of God,
Gentle mother of the Queen of heaven,
Grandmother of Our Savior,
Beloved of Jesus, Mary, and Joseph,
Instrument of the Holy Spirit,
Richly endowed with God's grace,
Example of piety and patience in suffering,
Mirror of obedience,
Ideal of pure womanhood,
Protectress of virgins,
Model of Christian mothers,
Protectress of the married,
Guardian of children,
Support of Christian family life,
Help of the Church,

Mother of mercy,
Mother of confidence,
Friend of the poor,
Example of widows,
Health of the sick,
Cure of those who suffer from disease,
Mother of the infirm,
Light of the blind,
Speech of those who cannot speak,
Hearing of the deaf,
Consolation of the afflicted,
Comforter of the oppressed,
Joy of the Angels and Saints,
Refuge of sinners,
Harbor of salvation,
Patroness of a happy death,
Help of those who have recourse to you.

—Funeral Homily for My Mother—

Back in 1986 when I celebrated my first Mass here, I looked out and reminded people of all the connections St. Peter's has had for my family.

I see the Communion of Saints — the vision of the Church gathered around Christ — the Church, the saints — all the friends of the Lord.

And isn't that what we celebrate this morning — the great friend that Ann Brown was to each of us here?

Ultimately, however, we celebrate her friendship with Christ — for no one in my life has ever lived as closely in friendship with Christ as Ann Brown.

> A faithful friend is a sturdy shelter —
> And gracious lips prompt friendly greetings.

I chose this reading from Sirach — not one generally used for a funeral liturgy. I chose it because I cannot think of a passage that better describes the life of Ann Brown.

> A faithful friend is a sturdy shelter.
> He that has found one has found a treasure.

Now what do I say from here.

I can hear her saying, "Tim, keep it short. Keep it simple. My friends prefer that. No theologizing. No one wants that today."

You are right, Mother. We learned our theology from the way you lived out your Catholic faith. We learned all that one could ever learn about friendship with Christ from your friendship with Him. You incorporated the Gospel into your daily life. Christianity was not a concept — not an idea — it was a lived-out principle every single day of your life.

Mother, thank you for teaching me about priesthood. You taught me from a very early age, driving me to Mass here for the 6:00 a.m. You taught me compassion. I think of all the ways you taught Christian faith in action. I think of you, and flowers, gifts, golf and bridge, great desserts, wonderful hors d'oeuvres, come to mind. And always your great laugh, heart to heart, with your friends.

No matter how sick you were or tired or ravaged by the diabetes and heart disease, you took in the words of the Lord: "This is my commandment. Love one another as I have loved you. No one has greater love than this, to lay down one's life for one's friend."

A faithful friend is beyond price.

This past week I had the privilege of taking you home from the hospital. I took you back into the same house to which you carried me home from the same hospital 47 years ago. We came full circle last week.

I looked at you smiling through pain and weakness, cracking a joke and attempting to take care of me for the last time. The word that comes to mind is resilience.

Resilience is the ability to cope with the setbacks life presents, and to draw on inner strengths of optimism, hope, determination, and great faith. Resilient persons are able to see life, no matter what happens, as holding good cards. And playing even a poor hand well.

I can remember you playing bridge, Mother, on more than one occasion playing a poor hand well. To me, that describes it all. Your resilience was absolutely inspiring to all of us.

It was grace — a real gift from God — and you played that hand well. And didn't you pick that up from the Lord Himself? Christ Himself is the Living Resilience.

When I received the news that your heart had finally given out, I said my prayer to the Sacred Heart.

Your heart had given out and you had given away everything in it. There was nothing left to give.

Your physical heart gave out, but not your heart united with Christ. Your resilient heart is now beating eternally with the Heart of Jesus Christ.

There were so many ways your heart was linked to the Sacred Heart — all your daily acts of kindness and all the good works you performed. All of us here today carry those memories of you in our hearts, forever linked through the Sacred Heart.

Hank Hilton asked me to imagine what you said to the Lord when you met Him for the first time, face to face.

I thought for a minute. I realized that it wasn't what you said to each other, but that you connected with each other — heart to heart. That's how I see you with the Lord.

Now, Mother, you can rest that heart of yours. Rest in the heart of God. Rest and enjoy all that you hold dear in your heart.

Eighty-one years ago Ann Schmidt was carried as an infant into this very church. She was brought to the beautiful Baptismal font that you see on the side of this altar. She died with Christ that day in 1919. She would later make her First Confession and First Communion in this church. She would be confirmed here and celebrate her marriage to Bernard Brown here on July 3, 1943. Her parents and my father's parents both were married here as well and spent their entire lives praying in this church.

Today we release her to St. Peter. For the final time in this holy place.

May 25, 2000

—Salve Regina—

Hail, Holy Queen,
Mother of mercy
Our life, our sweetness and our hope!
To you do we cry, poor banished children of Eve
To you do we send our sighs, mourning and weeping in
this valley of tears.
Turn then, most gracious advocate, your eyes of mercy
toward us.
And after this, our exile, show unto us the blessed fruit
of your womb, Jesus.
O clement, O loving, O sweet Virgin Mary.
O Mother of Jesus, at Golgotha you felt his pain; your
arms received his broken body.
Pray for us in our sorrowful days!

reconciliation

—Psalm 51—

1. Have mercy upon me, O God, according to thy lovingkindness: according unto the multitude of thy tender mercies blot out my transgressions.

2. Wash me thoroughly from mine iniquity, and cleanse me from my sin.

3. For I acknowledge my transgressions: and my sin is ever before me.

4. Against thee, thee only, have I sinned, and done this evil in thy sight: that thou mightest be justified when thou speakest, and be clear when thou judgest.

10. Create in me a clean heart, O God; and renew a right spirit within me.

11. Cast me not away from thy presence; and take not thy holy spirit from me.

12. Restore unto me the joy of thy salvation; and uphold me with thy free spirit.

15. O Lord, open thou my lips; and my mouth shall shew forth thy praise.

—An Act of Contrition—

O my God, I am heartily sorry for having offended thee. I detest all my sins because of thy just punishment, but most of all because they offend thee, my God, who art all good and deserving of all my love.

I firmly resolve with the help of thy grace to sin no more and to avoid the near occasion of sin.

Amen.

My parents taught me this prayer when I was young. They prayed this Act of Contrition, and I grew up praying this. Now I pray it for them. I think back on this thread of continuity through my family – all of us asking for forgiveness. This thread of connection to each other as I continue to ask the Lord's forgiveness.

—Late Have I Loved You—
St. Augustine

Late have I loved you, O beauty ever ancient, ever new!
Late have I loved you.
And behold, you were within, and I without,
  and without I sought you.
And deformed, I ran after those forms of beauty
  you have made.
You were with me, and I was not with you,
  those things held me back from you,
  things whose only being was to be in you.
You called; you cried;
  and you broke through my deafness.
You flashed; you shone;
  and you chased away my blindness.
You became fragrant;
  and I inhaled and sighed for you.
I tasted, and now hunger and thirst for you.
You touched me; and I burned for your embrace.

—Fix Your Eyes on the Crucified—
Teresa of Avila

Fix your eyes on the crucified and everything will become smaller for you.

—Prayer Before the Crucifix—

Behold, O good and gentle, I cast myself
Upon my knees in your sight and with all the ardor
Of my soul I pray and beseech you to impress upon
My heart lively sentiments of faith, hope, and love,
With true repentance for my sins and a firm purpose
Of amendment, while with deep affection and grief of
Soul I consider and contemplate your five wounds,
Having before my eyes the words which David your
Prophet said of you my good Jesus, they have pierced
My hands and feet.

They have numbered all my bones.

my father

—Psalm 116—

The grace of a happy death. My father died of a sudden heart attack in May 1983. Sudden – after dinner. He died in his sleep. I was 30 years old. He was 62. We were both too young.

3.   The sorrows of death compassed me, and the pains of hell gat hold upon me: I found trouble and   sorrow.

4.   Then called I upon the name of the Lord; O Lord, I beseech thee, deliver my soul.

5.   Gracious is the Lord, and righteous; yea, our God is merciful.

6.   The Lord preserveth the simple: I was brought low; and He helped me.

7.   Return unto thy rest, O my soul; for the Lord hath dealt bountifully with thee.

8.   For thou hast delivered my soul from death, mine eyes from tears, and my feet from falling.

9.   I will walk before the Lord in the land of the living.

10. I believed, therefore have I spoken: I was greatly afflicted:

13. I will take the cup of salvation, and call upon the name of the Lord.

14. I will pay my vows unto the Lord now in the presence of all his people.

15. Precious in the sight of the Lord is the death of his saints.

—Sirach 3: 2-6, 12-14—

For the Lord honors a father above his children,
And he confirms a mother's right over her children.

Those who honor their father atone for sins, and those
who respect their mother are like those who lay up treasure.

Those who honor their father will have joy in their own
children, and when they pray they will be heard.

Those who respect their father will have long life,
And those who honor their mother obey the Lord.

My child, help your father in his old age,
And do not grieve him as long as he lives;
Even if his mind fails, be patient with him;
Because you have all your faculties do not despise him.

For kindness to a father will not be forgotten,
And will be credited to you against your sins.

—Litany of St. Joseph—

Patron of a happy death – I pray to the foster father of Jesus and remember my own dad.

St. Joseph,
Renowned offspring of David,
Light of Patriarchs,
Spouse of the Mother of God,
Chaste guardian of the Virgin,
Foster father of the Son of God,
Watchful defender of Christ,
Head of the Holy Family,
Joseph most just,
Joseph most pure,
Joseph most prudent,
Joseph most courageous,
Joseph most obedient,
Joseph most faithful,
Mirror of patience,
Lover of poverty,
Model of all who labor,
Glory of family life,
Guardian of virgins,
Mainstay of families,
Solace of the afflicted,
Hope of the sick,
Patron of the dying,
Terror of demons,
Protector of the Holy Church.   *Hear our prayer.*

—Letter to My Father—

Our memorobilia truly capture a life. I found this letter among my father's effects. It says a great deal about him and his capacity to relate to a range of people from various religious backgrounds.

June 19, 1963

Dear Bernie:

I'm sorry that Bernie and I weren't able to spend more time with you and your family yesterday, but hope that all went well.

Originally I had planned to mail the enclosed to your home for your two children, but when I learned you would be in New York I decided to hold them pending your arrival.

The enclosed were blessed during what must have been one of Pope John's final public appearances, when my wife and I were in Rome last month. So perhaps beyond being blessed they also capture a fleeting moment of time in San Pietro Square when a man lived whose personality projected beyond all religions and whose humanity and understanding was a tangible bridge between all beliefs.

As you know, Bernie, I am not a Catholic. But I believe in Pope John as many hundreds of thousands of other non-Catholics did, and I hope that your children will feel the added significance of these medals blessed by this great man. Soon they will be striking the new face of a new Pontiff on medallions to be sold in the stores of Vatican City, and new tourists will come again to the Eternal City and buy them for remembered friends in the sunlight of St. Peter's. But these particular two, they will forever retain the features of a great and glowing leader of all men.

Best Wishes.

Cordially,
Dick

—Snapshots—

Great memories of my parents' lives together as glimpsed in this golf card. A snapshot of a great day in the summer of 1964 when my father got a hole-in-one. My parents – their friends – sunshine – laughter – golf. A life well-lived.

HDCP	YARDS	PAR	J.Beason	B.Brown	WE	HOLE	THEY	A.Brown	E.Beason	PAR	YARDS
7	400	4	5	5		1		7	8	5	400
13	310	4	6	5		2		7	8	4	310
3	445	4	5	5		3		7	8	5	425
9	340	4	6	6		4		6	6	4	340
1	511	5	6	6		5		8	8	5	461
17	152	3	4	3		6		5	6	3	152
11	347	4	6	5		7		7	7	4	347
5	490	5	7	5		8		7	9	5	420
15	152	3	4	3		9		6	4	3	152
	2147	36	48	43	OUT		60	64	38		3017
12	395	4	6	6		10		8	8	5	375
14	353	4	5	5		11		7	7	4	353
2	520	5	6	6		12		8	8	5	480
16	342	4	5	5		13		6	6	4	212
6	370	4	6	5		14		7	7	5	370
10	393	4	6	6		15		7	10	4	393
8	358	4	6	4		16		7	8	4	358
18	132	3	5	(1)		17		3	6	3	132
4	406	4	4	6		18		8	7	5	406
	3267	36	49	44	IN		61	68	39		3119
	6414	72	97	87	OUT		121	132	77		6136

SCORER _____ DATE Aug. 9 '64

ATTEST B. Brown

E. Beason

prayers for the dying

—Psalm 102—

1.   Hear my prayer, O Lord, and let my cry come unto thee.

2.   Hide not thy face from me in the day when I am in trouble; incline thine ear unto me: in the day when I call answer me speedily.

3.   For my days are consumed like smoke, and my bones are burned as an hearth.

4.   My heart is smitten, and withered like grass; so that I forget to eat my bread.

5.   By reason of the voice of my groaning my bones cleave to my skin.

6.   I am like a pelican of the wilderness: I am like an owl of the desert.

7.   I watch, and am as a sparrow alone upon the house top.

11. My days are like a shadow that declineth; and I am withered like grass.

—Prayer for the Dying—

O My God, I offer thee all the holy Masses which will be said this day throughout the whole world for poor sinners who are now in their death agony and who will die this day. May the Precious Blood of our Savior Jesus Christ obtain for them mercy.

Prayer to be said at the side of the dying:

I love God with my whole heart, and more especially I desire to love the Lord my God with the love with which all the saints have loved him.

I am heartily sorry for all the sins whatsoever I have committed against my Lord and against my neighbor – all for the love of God.

I also, for the love of God, forgive with all my heart all those who have in any way offended me or shown themselves my enemies.

I ask pardon of all whom I have offended in word or act.

I desire to bear with patience, on account of my sins, all the sufferings and discomforts of my sickness.

I resolve if God restores me to health, to avoid sin and be faithful to God's commandments.

— Anonymous

—The Next Thing—

Being with the dying. Readying yourself for what has become only a matter of hours or days you wonder, "How can I be present? It is too much. How will I be able to manage after they are gone?" It is in that moment I think about Father Joe Whelan.

Father Joe Whelan, S.J., was diagnosed with cancer several years ago. He had been Provincial Superior for the Maryland Province and then Regional Assistant in Rome. Before he died he was interviewed by America magazine and asked to sum up his life. He said, "simply nothing will do except prayer." And then he added, "Grace. And when you think about your life and you look at next week coming up or at the month you say, I just don't see how I can get through all that, but can you do the next thing. If the next thing were to listen to me for another twenty minutes, could you do that? Ordinarily you'd be able to say, 'Yeah, I can do that.' So I find that the prayer most frequently said is, 'With your help, dear Lord, I can do the next thing.'"

With your help, Lord, I can do the next thing.

—St. Therese—

Let us profit from our one moment of suffering.

Let us see only each moment. A moment is a treasure.

One act of love will make us know Jesus better. It will bring us closer to him during the whole of eternity.

For me, prayer is an upward leap of the heart, an untroubled glance toward heaven, and a cry of gratitude and love which I utter from the depths of sorrow as well as from the heights of joy.

—Comfort—
Janet Erskine Stuart, RSCJ

I know that when the stress has grown too strong,
Thou wilt be there.
I know that though the waiting seems so long,
Thou hearest prayer.
I know that through the crash of falling worlds,
Thou holdest me.
I know that life and death and all are thine,
Eternally!

—Stay With Me—

Stay with me
This evening
The last evening of my life
The last evening of the world
Stay with me
With your grace and goodness
With your holy word and sacraments
Stay with me
When I am threatened with fears and anxiety
When I am troubled with doubt
And insecurity
When I am lonesome
When I am sick
When I am dying
Stay with me
And with my family
When we are happy
When we are sad
When we succeed.
Stay with me.

– Anonymous

—You Were for Me an Anchor—

I had a friend who suffered from Lou Gehrig's disease (A.L.S.).
Preparing for death, she sent her close friends this message:

I wanted to let you know how I feel so even now I will be
known for my bluntness!

You have journeyed with me on this ocean voyage.

We have visited islands of serenity;
Experienced storms at sea;
Been treated to exhilarating crests of the waves;
And awesome sunrise and sunsets at sea.

We have had times of the "Hum Drum" just waiting to
catch fish.

And in all of these varied experiences
We have been there for each other
And that has helped me to be who I am.

Your love has nourished, challenged, and supported me
and hopefully I have done that for you.

Thank you for the times when you were for me an
anchor. Oars...A boat...Sails...And a sailing companion...And hopefully I have done that for you...

The captain of the sea has invited me (I wouldn't be going if He didn't!!!) to go across to the other side so that I may rest in the glory and wonder of His presence; and abide in His gentle love.

This is what enables me to say my final fiat…Without the three dots, [Thérèse purposely inscribed three dots between Pater and Fiat on her ring at final vows as she anticipated a lifelong need to "argue" with God's terms of her vocation].

So it is not good-bye that I say but…

…Hasta La Vista

…Or I'll see you soon.

— Thérèse Wenzel

heaven

—Psalm 89—

2.   For I have said, Mercy shall be built up forever:
      thy faithfulness shalt thou establish in the very
      heavens.

3.   I have made a covenant with my chosen, I have
      sworn unto David, my servant,

4.   Thy seed will I establish for ever, and build up
      thy throne to all generations.

9.   And the heavens shall praise thy wonders, O
      Lord: thy faithfulness also in the congregations
of
      the saints.

13.   Thou hast a mighty arm: strong is thy hand, and
      high is thy right hand.

14.   Justice and judgment are the habitation of thy
      throne: mercy and truth shall go before thy
      face.

15.   Blessed is the people that know the joyful sound:
      they shall walk, O Lord, in the light of thy coun-
      tenance.

16.   In thy name shall they rejoice all the day: and in
      thy righteousness shall they be exalted.

—Nigerian Novices—

This letter was sent by me last summer to the Jesuits of the Maryland Province when I was told that two Jesuit novices had died suddenly.

Prayer for the Graces of St. Stanislaus Kostka:

O God, Who among the many wonders of Your wisdom
endow some, even in tender years, with
the grace of ripest holiness: grant unto us,
we beseech You, after the pattern of blessed
Stanislaus, to be instant in good works, and thus to
make speed to enter into everlasting rest. Amen.

Dear Brothers in Christ:

May Christ's Peace be with you. It was with great sadness that I learned yesterday of the death by drowning of two novices, Anthony Konwea and Henry Okparajiego, from the Novitiate in Benin City, Nigeria. I ask all of you to join me in prayers for their fellow novices, their families, and for George Quickley, their novice master.

When I pray, "Grant them eternal rest, O Lord, and let your perpetual light shine upon them," let my words be only the echo of the prayer of love that they themselves are speaking for me in the silence of eternity: "O Lord, grant unto him whom we love in your Love now as never before, grant unto him after his life's struggle your eternal rest, and let your perpetual light shine also upon him, as it does upon us."

O my soul, never forget the dead. O God of all the living, do not forget me, the dead one, but come one day to be my life, as you are theirs.
— Karl Rahner

We pray for the departed because we love them in the love that comes from God. And believing them to be nearer God than we are, we are sure that they pray for us more strongly within that same love. To ask the departed to pray for us and ourselves to pray for them is a natural expression of our solidarity with them in the redemptive love of God in Christ. God vividly speaks to us in those who shared our humanity and yet are transformed into images of Christ.

It can be difficult for those left behind when someone leaves this world so abruptly, and to lose two men in this way is that much harder. All of our friends who have died become part of our Communion of Saints to whom we can then turn. This personal connection to the Communion of Saints is a real source of courage to me.

Jesus, to die in the Society, or may you take me before letting me leave it, or whatever is for your greater glory. I offer myself for the Society, blood and life.

- Francis Borgia

Both prayer and the Psalms have offered me a great deal of consolation in times of loss. Let us unite in heart and minds with our brothers in Nigeria as they face the loss of their fellow novices. And pray that our Blessed Mother will throw the mantle of her love over them and bring them the consolation they need. Be assured that you are all in my prayers.

—John 11: 25-26—

Jesus told her, "I am the resurrection and the life; whoever believes in me, even if he dies, will live, and everyone who lives and believes in me will never die. Do you believe this?"

—Restless Hearts—
Saint Augustine

Lord, you created us for yourself and our hearts are restless until they rest in you. Please show us how to love you with all our heart and our neighbor as ourself. Teach us to be practical about loving one another in you and for you as you desire. Show us our immediate neighbor today; call our attention to the needs of others. Remind us that you count as done to you what we do for one another, and that our turning away from one another is really turning our backs on you. Make us know, love and serve you in this life and be happy forever in the next in union with all our sisters and brothers, children of a common God.

—Philippians 3:20—

For our conversation is in heaven; from whence also we look for the Saviour, the Lord Jesus Christ.

—Death Is Nothing At All—

Death is nothing at all, I have only slipped away into the
    next room.
Whatever we were to each other, that we are still.
Call me by my own familiar name.
Speak to me in the easy way which you always used.
Laugh as we always laughed at the little jokes we enjoyed
    together.
Play, smile, think of me, pray for me.
Let my name be the household word that it always was.
Let it be spoken without effort.
Life means all that it ever meant, it is the same as it ever
    was; there is absolutely unbroken continuity.
Why should I be out of your mind because I am out of
    your sight?
I am but waiting for you, for an interval, somewhere very
    near, just around the corner.
All is well.
Nothing is past; nothing is lost.
One brief moment and all will be as it was before — only
    better, infinitely happier and forever — we will all be
    one together with Christ.

Carmelite Monastery,
Waterford, Ireland

—Sing, Then, But Keep Going—
Saint Augustine

O the happiness of the heavenly alleluia, sung in security, in fear of no adversity! We shall have no enemies in heaven, we shall never lose a friend, God's praises are sung both there and here, but here they are sung in anxiety, there, in security; here they are sung by those destined to die, there, by those destined to live forever; here they are sung in hope, there, in hope's fulfillment; here they are sung by wayfarers, there, by those living in their own country.

So, then, let us sing now, not in order to enjoy a life of leisure, but in order to lighten our labors. You should sing as wayfarers do — sing; but continue your journey. Do not be lazy, but sing to make your journey more enjoyable. Sing, but keep going. What do I mean by keep going? Keep on making progress. This progress, however, must be in virtue; for there are some, the Apostle warns, whose only progress is in vice. If you make progress, you will be continuing your journey, but be sure that your progress is in virtue, true faith and right living. Sing then, but keep going!

—Our Home is Heaven—
John Vianney

Our home is heaven.

On Earth, we are like travelers staying at a hotel. When one is away, one is always thinking of going home.

—2 Corinthians 5: 1, 6-10—

For we know that if our earthly dwelling, a tent, should be destroyed, we have a building from God, a dwelling not made with hands, eternal in heaven. So we are always courageous, although we know that while we are at home in the body we are away from the Lord, for we walk by faith, not by sight. Yet we are courageous, and we would rather leave the body and go home to the Lord. Therefore, we aspire to please him, whether we are at home or away. For we must all appear before the judgment seat of Christ, so that each one may recompense, according to what he did in the body, whether good or evil.

God's love

—Psalm 90—

1. Lord, thou hast been our dwelling place in all generations.

2. Before the mountains were brought forth, or ever thou hadst formed the earth and the world, even from everlasting to everlasting, thou art God.

3. Thou turnest man to destruction; and sayest, Return, ye children of men.

4. For a thousand years in thy sight are but as yesterday when it is past, and as a watch in the night.

5. Thou carriest them away as with a flood; they are as a sleep: in the morning they are like grass which groweth up.

6. In the morning it flourisheth, and groweth up; in the evening it is cut down, and withereth.

7. For we are consumed by thine anger, and by thy wrath are we troubled.

8. Thou hast set our iniquities before thee, our secret sins in the light of thy countenance.

9.   For all our days are passed away in thy wrath: we spend our years as a tale that is told.

10.   The days of our years are threescore years and ten; and if by reason of strength they be fourscore years, yet is their strength labor and sorrow; for it is soon cut off, and we fly away.

11.   Who knoweth the power of thine anger? Even according to thy fear, so is thy wrath.

12.   So teach us to number our days, that we may apply our hearts unto wisdom.

13.   Return, O Lord, how long? And let it repent thee concerning thy servants.

14.   O satisfy us early with thy mercy; that we may rejoice and be glad all our days.

15.   Make us glad according to the days wherein thou hast afflicted us, and the years wherein we have seen evil.

16.   Let thy work appear unto thy servants, and thy glory unto their children.

17.   And let the beauty of the Lord our God be upon us: and establish thou the work of our hands upon us; yea, the work of our hands establish thou it.

—Be Always Ours—
St. Patrick

May the strength of God pilot us.
May the strength of God preserve us.
May the wisdom of God instruct us.
May the hand of God protect us.
May the shield of God defend us..
May the host of God guard us against the snares of
    the evil one
And the temptation of the world.
May Christ be with us.
Christ above us.
Christ in us.
Christ before us.
May the salvation, O Lord,
Be always ours.
This day and for evermore.
Amen.

—On Love—
Thomas a Kempis

Love is a mighty power, a great and complete good.
Love alone lightens every burden,
and makes rough places smooth.
It bears every hardship as though it were nothing,
and renders all bitterness sweet and acceptable.

Nothing is sweeter than love,
Nothing stronger, Nothing higher,
Nothing wider, Nothing more pleasant,
Nothing fuller or better in heaven or earth;
for love is born of God.

Love flies, runs and leaps for joy.
It is free and unrestrained.
Love knows no limits,
but ardently transcends all bounds.
Love feels no burden, takes no account of toil,
attempts things beyond its strength.

Love sees nothing as impossible,
for it feels able to achieve all things.
It is strange and effective,
while those who lack love faint and fail.

Love is not fickle and sentimental,
nor is it intent on vanities.
Like a living flame and burning torch,
it surges upward and surely surmounts every obstacle.

—The Love of My God—

Saint Augustine

What is it that I love when I love my God?
It is a certain light that I love and
melody and fragrance and embrace that
I love when I love my God — a light,
melody, fragrance, food embrace of the
God-within, where, for my soul, that
shines which space does not contain;
that sounds which time does not sweep away;
that is fragrant which the breeze does
not dispel; and that tastes sweet which,
fed upon, is not diminished; and that
clings close which no satiety disparts —
This is what I love when I love my God.

—Shine Through Me—
Cardinal Newman

Dear Lord, shine through me, and be so in me that every soul I come in contact with may feel your perseverance in my soul. Let them look up and see no longer me, but only you, O Lord. Stay with me, and then I shall begin to shine as you do; so to shine as to be a light to others. Let me thus praise you in the way you love best, by shining on those around me.

—Two Things—

Jesus promises two things: your life has meaning and you're going to live forever. If you get a better offer, take it.

— Gene Walsh (1911-1989)

peace

—Psalm 46—

1.   God is our refuge and strength, a very present help in trouble.

2.   Therefore will not we fear, though the earth be removed, and though the mountains be carried into the midst of the sea;

3.   Though the waters thereof roar and be troubled, though the mountains shake with the swelling thereof.

4.   There is a river, the streams whereof shall make glad the city of God, the holy place of the tabernacles of the most High.

—Peace—
St. Francis de Sales

Do not look forward to what might happen tomorrow.
The same everlasting Father who cares for us today,
will take care of you tomorrow and everyday.
Either He will shield you from suffering or He will
give you unfailing strength to bear it.
Be at peace then and put aside all anxious thoughts
and imaginations.

—Let Us Go in Peace—
St. Therese

Let us go forward in peace,
our eyes upon heaven,
the only one goal of our labours.

—Lord Support Us—
Cardinal Newman

May He support us all the day long till the shades lengthen and the evening comes

And the busy world is hushed and the fever of life is over and our work is done

Then in His mercy may He give us a safe lodging and a holy rest and peace at the last.

—Deep Peace—
Irish Blessing

Deep peace of the running wave to you,
Deep peace of the flowing air to you,

Deep peace of the shining stars to you,
Deep peace of the quiet earth to you,

Deep peace of the Son of Peace to you.

—John 14: 1-12—

"Do not let your hearts be troubled. You have faith in God; faith also in me. In my Father's house there are many dwelling places. If there were not, would I have told you that I am going to prepare a place for you? And if I go and prepare a place for you, I will come back again and take you to myself, so that where I am you may also be. Where I am going you know the way." Thomas said to him, "Master, we do not know where you are going; how can we know the way?" Jesus said to him, "I am the way and the truth and the life. No one comes to the Father except through me. If you know me, then you will also know my Father. From now on you do know him and have seen him." Philip said to him, "Master show us the Father, and that will be enough for us." Jesus said to him, "Have I been with you for so long a time and you still do not know me, Philip? Whoever has seen me has seen the Father. How can you say, 'Show us the Father'? Do you not believe that I am in the Father and the Father is in me? The words that I speak to you I do not speak on my own. The Father who dwells in me is doing his works. Believe me that I am in the Father and the Father is in me, or else, believe because of the works themselves. Amen, amen, I say to you, whoever believes in me will do the works that I do, and will do greater ones than these, because I am going to the Father."

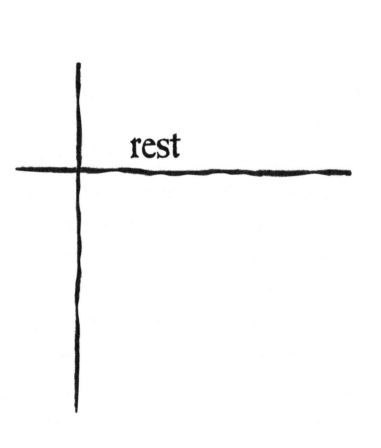

rest

—Psalm 55—

1. Give ear to my prayer, O God; and hide not thy-
    self from my supplication.

2. Attend unto me, and hear me: I mourn in my
    complaint, and make a noise;

3. Because of the voice of the enemy, because of the
    oppression of the wicked: for they cast iniquity
    upon me, and in wrath they hate me.

4. My heart is sore pained within me: and the ter-
    rors of death are fallen upon me.

5. Fearfulness and trembling are come upon me,
    and horror hath overwhelmed me.

6. And I said, Oh that I had wings, like a dove! for
    then would I fly away, and be at rest.

—Prayer of St. Francis Xavier—

It is not Your promised Heaven
that moves me, Lord, to love You.
It is not the fear of Hell,
that forces me to fear You.
What moves me, Lord, is You, Lord,
fixed on the Cross and mocked.
What moves me is Your wounded body,
the insults and Your death.
What moves me really is Your love, so that
were there no Heaven, I would love You still.
Were there no Hell, I would fear You still.
For me to love You, You need nothing to give.
For even if I did not hope, as indeed I hope,
even so I would love You as indeed I love.

—Sun Without Rain—

God has not promised sun without rain,
Joy without sorrow,
Peace without pain.
But God has promised strength for the day,
Rest for the labor,
Light for the way,
Grace for the trials,
Help from above,
Unfailing sympathy,
Undying love.

—Funeral of Diane Geppi-Aikens—
July, 2003

Diane Geppi-Aikens was an inspirational leader not only to the women who played lacrosse for her at Loyola College in Baltimore, Maryland, for fifteen years but also to anyone who had the privilege of knowing her. She lost an eight-year battle with brain cancer during the summer of 2003, after having coached the women's lacrosse team to the NCAA semi-finals. When Diane first learned in December of 2002 that her cancer had returned and that she might not live until Memorial Day, she set two goals: to lead her team to the NCAA Final Four, and to see her son Michael, the eldest of her four children, graduate from high school the last day of May. Both of those goals Diane attained. She has been a source of inspiration for all as she faced her disease with toughness tempered by humor.

Speaking for all of us gathered here this morning, I want to express our profound sympathy and support for Diane's father and mother, John and Catherine Geppi; to her grandmother, Marie Meyers; to Diane's sisters Patty and Carolyn; to her beautiful and wonderful children, Michael, Jessica, Melissa and Shannon; and to the children's father, Bob Aikens and to Andrea, Diane's devoted friend.

Words. Words are what we in an academic community are usually so very good with. But here, now, at times like this words have a way of eluding us. Words fail. Words seem terribly inadequate.

We even fear, do we not, that our meager attempts to

speak of words of sympathy and consolidation will seem too facile, and that we will not seem sensitive enough to the fact that those whom we would hope to comfort with these words are in deep pain and they are sore at heart.

Oh, some words don't fail; some words take on a meaning not fully known before. Words like: shock, loss, grief, absence, sorrow; even words like: anger and doubt. When we lose someone whom we have loved and whom we have cherished and admired so immensely, the whole vocabulary of grief becomes real.

For months, now, we have been saying to one another: "This should not be happening." That, sadly, it does happen confounds and perplexes us. We pray that we will have faith enough to believe that, in all of this suffering and loss, God's fatherly care for his daughter Diane is a reality, even though we may not see it now through our tears. But here and now pain and deep sorrow are what we know. A daughter, a mother, a dear friend, a beloved coach and mentor is gone.

Comfort. Comfort is the word that describes what we wish to give here this morning. We want our presence and prayers to give comfort to Diane's family and to each other. But it is even hard for comfort to root itself within us when so many other painful emotions rush about within.

We know that time will slowly ease the pain. Not that we will forget, but time will bring so many fond memories of Diane's life. And those memories will make us ever grateful for what a gift it has been to have had Diane Geppi-Aikens as part of our lives.

Energy. Perhaps what was hardest for those who knew her best was to witness her great energy diminished. To have seen her on the lacrosse field as a player, to watch her pace the sideline during a game or to race her players in wind sprints at the end of practice was to glimpse the remarkable physical energy she possessed. Hers was the grace of the athlete — the economy of movement, the sureness in her physical presence — and always, always the awareness that the potential energy just beneath the surface could be unleashed at a moment's notice.

Just as impressive was her mental energy, her seemingly innate understanding of sports, her capacity to concentrate and to quickly assess a situation, whether it was during a game or with a personal challenge of one of the many players she mentored both on and off the field.

Even during the last difficult months when she was confined to a wheelchair, the intensity remained. During the final game of the season, when the team secured the top seeding in the NCAA tournament with its dramatic come-from-behind victory over Maryland, the referees made a questionable yellow card call on one of the Loyola players. There was some discussion on the field, and just as matters seemed to have settled, out came Diane in the wheelchair. The crowd went wild.

And then, two days after the disappointing loss to Princeton in the national semifinal, when no one would have blamed her for taking some time off to rest, she was off to Pennsylvania to recruit for four days, watching high school girls play lacrosse games on muddy fields in chilly downpour. Energy.

Spirit. If you have taken a look at the voluminous message on the Diane Aikens website, which was established just after her diagnosis last December, you undoubtedly would be struck by the number of persons who feel that Diane touched their lives in significant ways. Former players, opposing coaches, parents, colleagues, friends — all credit her with inspiring them to reach for their best.

And if you called at her home on Brook Avenue you would begin to see why people felt this way about Diane. From the moment you walked up to the front door, you could see that the house is filled to overflowing with inspirational sayings, little plaques and mementos, greeting cards and homemade signs — constant reminders to keep looking forward, to seek out the best in people, to have faith and trust in God. All of these are crammed into spaces surrounded by photos of her four beautiful children and her wonderfully close family.

Her great spirit filled that house, just as it filled her office. And if you have been to either, you know that they were extremely cluttered places, the sayings and photos vying for space with books and trophies and magazines and the thousand details of daily life. But even in that clutter, if you asked Diane to find something, she could always put her finger on it immediately.

In that, I find a clue to her great success as a coach. She did not force her players to fit into a mold. She let them be themselves, thirty or forty women with all the clutter of their individual personalities, their strengths and vulnerabilities. She knew them one by one. And armed with that knowledge, Diane always seemed to be able to find the right person for the right place at the right time.

And they loved her for that, and they played all the harder, and they won. For them, as for all those who wrote messages on the website, Diane herself was the right person at the right place, at the right time. For Loyola College, she was the right person, at the right place, at the right time. Spirit.

Will. With her diagnosis this past December, Diane set three goals. She wanted to see her team play in its final televised game, she wanted to go to the Final Four, and she wanted to see her oldest child, Michael, graduate from Calvert Hall. She achieved all of them.

For those of us who watched her coach this year, it would be easy to overlook the tremendous effort it must have taken to achieve all of these goals. She took the distractions of the local and national media in stride; she signed autographs on the sidelines for hours; she coached just as she always had. We knew she was tired, but she would not succumb; she defied her disease.

How did she manage to do it? We have all asked ourselves that question many times over the past several months. I suspect the answer is in one word: habit. The habit of a lifetime. It was always about her family, her friends, her players, her school. It was never about Diane.

And so all of these great memories of Diane will, we hope, slowly ease the pain. Faith and trust in God will also ease the pain. In the letter to the Romans, St. Paul teaches: "As Christ was raised from the dead by the glorious power of the Father, so also will we set out on a new life" (Romans, 6, 4). This is the great promise, this is the Father's word to each one of us, sealed in the blood of His Son: that even in the dark passage of death, nothing "will be able to separate us from the love of God in Christ Jesus our Lord" (Romans, 8,39). We will not be lost; we will be in His hands; having loved us into life, His love will be with us forever.

God's word of promise must be our comfort now. And God's word is not that our human lives will be forever. God's word is not that we shall not die. God's word is that His new life is eternal and that nothing will ever separate us from His love.

In the first reading from the Book of Wisdom, we read, "The souls of the just are in the hands of God" (3, 1). To believe this is to do far more than to hope that, after our time here on earth, there will be "something" rather than nothing. To believe that the "souls of the just are in the hands of God" is to believe that our lives here on earth are only a beginning, a prelude to what the loving God has prepared for those who love him and do His works. This is not an understanding of the mind; it is an understanding of the heart. It is a conviction that love follows upon love – and that, as God's creatures, you and I can never cease to be once God has loved us into being. It is a conviction and a promise offered to each one of us: the young and the old, women and men, the rich and the poor, the powerful and the powerless alike.

This is the conviction that powerfully sustained Diane in her illness and in her dying. It is the promise that is now fulfilled in Diane's new life in God.

With a potential sense of gratitude for the many blessings of her life, we now commit this gracious and splendid woman, Diane Geppi-Aikens to the tender miracles of the Lord.

And as we do so, let us listen to Isaiah the Prophet as he reminds us that the Lord God's care for his people is eternal:

"But now this is the word of the Lord,
The word of your creator:
'Have no fear,
I have called you by name, and you are my own.
When you pass through deep waters, I am with you;
when you pass through rivers
they will not sweep you away;
Walk through fire and you will not be scorched,
Through flames and they will not burn you.
For I am the Lord your God,
The Holy One of Israel, your deliverer.'"

– Rev. Harold E. Ridley, S.J.

—Anima Christi—

Soul of Christ, sanctify me.
Body of Christ, save me.
Blood of Christ, inebriate me.
Water from the side of Christ, wash me.
Passion of Christ, strengthen me.
O good Jesus, hear me.
Within thy wounds hide me.
Suffer me not to be separated from thee.
From the malicious enemy defend me.
In the hour of my death call me
and bid me come unto thee,
that with thy saints I may praise thee
for ever and ever. Amen.

—Cloud of Witnesses—
St. Bridget's Prayer

I should like a great lake of beer for the King of Kings.

I should like the angels of Heaven to be drinking it through time eternal.

I should like excellent meats of belief and pure piety.

I should like the men of heaven at my house.

I should like barrels of peace at their disposal.

I should like vessels of charity for distribution.

I should like for them cellars of mercy.

I should like cheerfulness to be in their drinking.

I should like Jesus to be there among them.

I should like the three Mary's of illustrious renown to be with us.

I should like the people of heaven, the poor, to be gathered around us from all parts.

—The Still Point of the Turning World—

Excerpts from my letter to the friends of the Maryland Province on All Saints Day.

May Christ's Peace be with you.

November is traditionally the month to pray for the souls of the faithful departed. On All Souls Day we celebrate our ancestors, the people whose past carries our present, the people whose words still vibrate in our minds.

This communion of saints is the ongoing connection between the living and the dead. We have access to these souls through memory and hope. The primary memory of our Christian community occurs in the sacramental action of the Eucharist, where the memorial of Jesus' death and resurrection becomes a living reality in the lives of those who celebrate it. Cheered on by this great, richly varied cloud of witnesses, the church today takes its own steps on the path of discipleship as legacy for future generations.

As I write this, I am just beginning my six years of service as Provincial of the Maryland Province. I know how much your faithful support — your prayers, your service, and your financial help — has benefited the Province. I want to express my gratitude for your generous support of our training young Jesuits, caring for older and infirm Jesuits, and helping us sustain our many ministries in the United States and abroad.

Together let us pray at this time for our communion of saints who are, to use a beautiful metaphor, a shining river of stars spiraling out from the galaxy's center, the still point of the turning world who is God alone, to light a path through the darkness.

—Precious Lord, Take My Hand—
Text and tune by Thomas A. Dorsey

Refrain:
Precious Lord, take my hand,
Lead me on, let me stand,
I am tired, I am weak, I am worn;
Thru the storm, thru the night,
Lead me on to the light,
Take my hand, precious Lord,
Lead me home.

When my way grows drear, precious Lord, linger near,
When my life is almost gone,
Hear my cry, hear my call,
Hold my hand lest I fall;
Take my hand, precious Lord, Lead me home. Refrain.

When the darkness appears and then night draws near,
And the day is past and gone,
At the river I stand,
Guide my feet, hold my hand;
Take my hand, precious Lord, Lead me home. Refrain.

—Blessing of Light—

May the blessing of light be on you, light without and light within.

May the blessed sunlight shine on you and warm your heart till it glows like a great peat fire, so that the stranger may come and warm himself at it, and also a friend.

And may the light shine out of the two eyes of you, like a candle set in two windows of a house, bidding the wanderer to come in out of the storm.

And may the blessing of the rain be on you — the soft sweet rain.

May it fall upon your spirit so that all the little flowers may spring up, and shed their sweetness on the air. And may the blessing of the great rains be on you, may it beat upon your spirit and wash it fair and clean, and leave there many a shining pool where the blue of heaven shines, and sometimes a star.

And may the blessing of the earth be on you — the great round earth; may you ever have a kindly greeting for them you pass as you're going along the roads.

May the earth be soft under you when you rest out upon it, tired at the end of a day, and may it rest easy over you when, at last, you lay out under it; may it rest so lightly over you, that your soul may be off from under it quickly and up, and off, and on its way to God.

And now may the Lord bless you all, and bless you kindly.

— *Anonymous*

—Pray for Me—
St. Thomas More

Pray for me
As I will for thee
That we may merrily meet in heaven

—Eternal Rest—

Eternal rest,
grant unto them O Lord,
and let perpetual light shine upon them.
Requiem aeternam dona eis domine
et lux perpetua luceat eis.

Rest

Rest

Rest

—Bibliography—

Norris, Kathleen. The Psalms. With Commentary.
    New York: Riverhead Books, 1997.

The Holy Bible. The New American Bible.

William J. Young, S.J., translator. The Spiritual Journal
    of St. Ignatius Loyola. Woodstock, Maryland:
    Woodstock College Press, 1958.

CPSIA information can be obtained at www.ICGtesting.com
Printed in the USA
BVOW08s0142090416

443174BV00001B/9/P